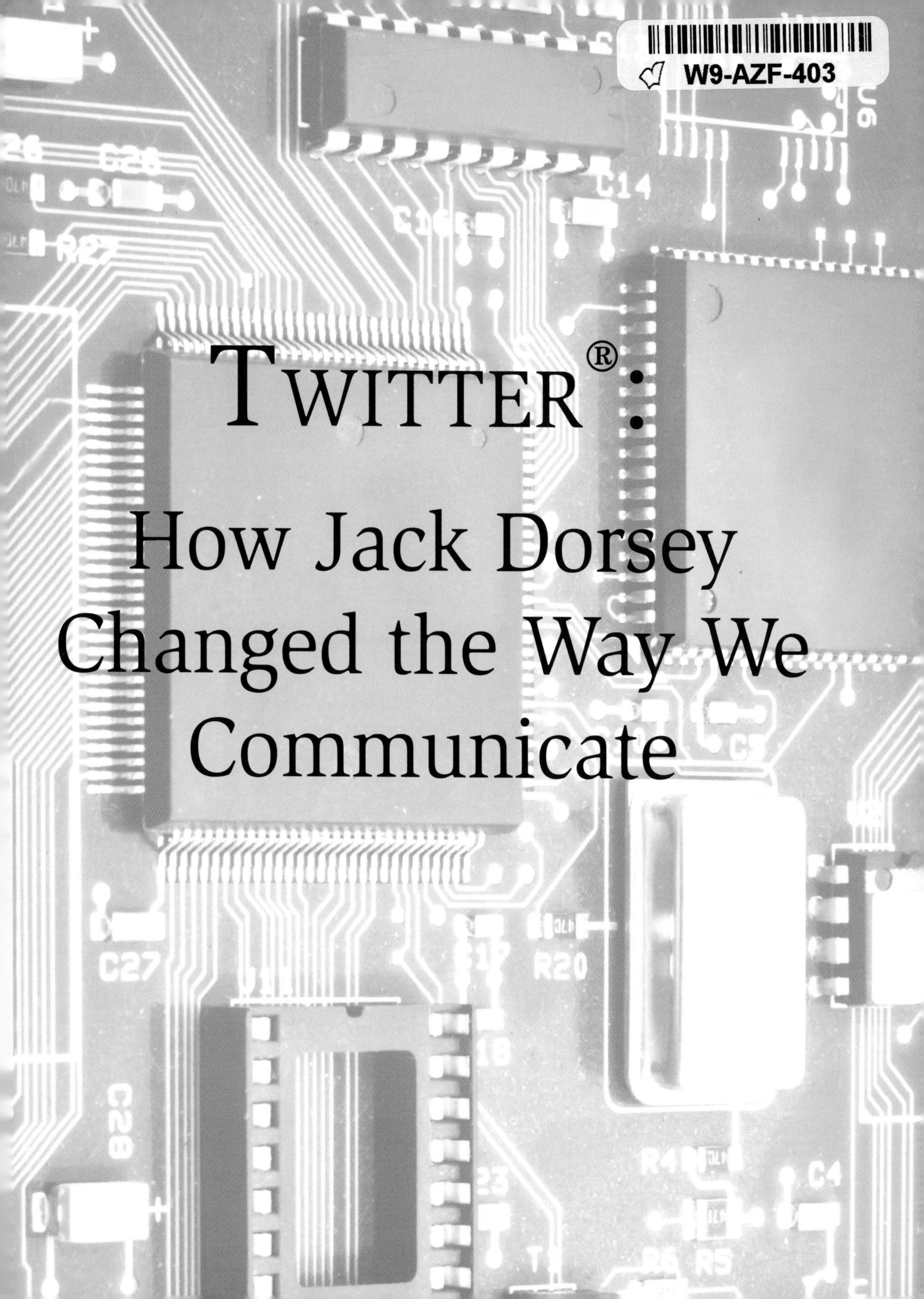

TWITTER®:

How Jack Dorsey Changed the Way We Communicate

WIZARDS OF TECHNOLOGY

Amazon®: How Jeff Bezos Built the World's Largest Online Store

Disney's Pixar®: How Steve Jobs Changed Hollywood

Facebook®: How Mark Zuckerberg Connected More Than a Billion Friends

Google®: How Larry Page & Sergey Brin Changed the Way We Search the Web

Instagram®: How Kevin Systrom & Mike Krieger Changed the Way We Take and Share Photos

Netflix®: How Reed Hastings Changed the Way We Watch Movies & TV

Pinterest®: How Ben Silbermann & Evan Sharp Changed the Way We Share What We Love

Tumblr®: How David Karp Changed the Way We Blog

Twitter®: How Jack Dorsey Changed the Way We Communicate

YouTube®: How Steve Chen Changed the Way We Watch Videos

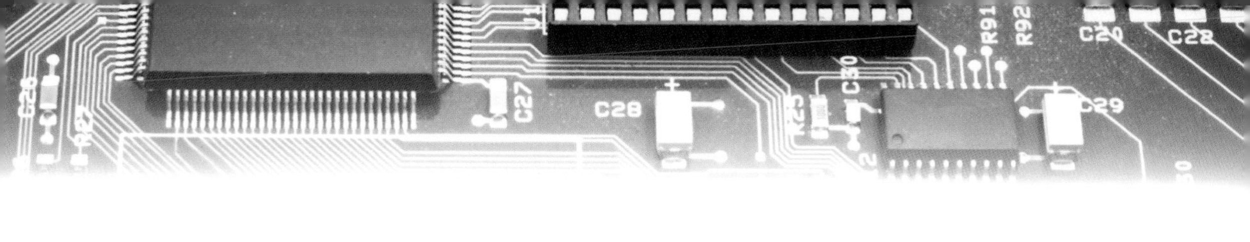

WIZARDS OF TECHNOLOGY

TWITTER®:
How Jack Dorsey Changed the Way We Communicate

CELICIA SCOTT

Mason Crest
450 Parkway Drive, Suite D
Broomall, PA 19008
www.masoncrest.com

Printed and bound in the USA.

First printing
9 8 7 6 5 4 3 2

Series ISBN: 978-1-4222-3178-4
ISBN: 978-1-4222-3187-6
ebook ISBN: 978-1-4222-8723-1

Library of Congress Cataloging-in-Publication Data

Scott, Celicia, 1957-
Twitter : how Jack Dorsey changed the way we communicate / Celicia Scott.
pages cm. — (Wizards of technology)
ISBN 978-1-4222-3187-6 (hardback) — ISBN 978-1-4222-3178-4 (series) — ISBN 978-1-4222-8723-1 (ebook) 1. Dorsey, Jack, 1976-—Juvenile literature. 2. Twitter (Firm)—Juvenile literature. 3. Twitter—Juvenile literature. 4. Microblogs—Juvenile literature. 5. Businessmen—United States—Biography—Juvenile literature. I. Title.
HM743.T95S36 2015
338.7'61004092—dc23
[B]

2014012233

CONTENTS

KEY ICONS TO LOOK FOR:

Text-Dependent Questions: These questions send the reader back to the text for more careful attention to the evidence presented there.

Words to Understand: These words with their easy-to-understand definitions will increase the reader's understanding of the text, while building vocabulary skills.

Series Glossary of Key Terms: This back-of-the book glossary contains terminology used throughout this series. Words found here increase the reader's ability to read and comprehend higher-level books and articles in this field.

Research Projects: Readers are pointed toward areas of further inquiry connected to each chapter. Suggestions are provided for projects that encourage deeper research and analysis.

Sidebars: This boxed material within the main text allows readers to build knowledge, gain insights, explore possibilities, and broaden their perspectives by weaving together additional information to provide realistic and holistic perspectives.

Words to Understand

entrepreneur: Someone who starts a new business.
dispatch: The organization that answers emergency calls and sends police or emergency personnel to respond.
enthusiast: Someone very interested in something.
application: A computer program designed to do a job.
revolutionary: Having to do with a dramatically new way of doing things.
impediment: Something that's in your way, keeping you from doing something.
impromptu: Spontaneous; not planned in advance.
efficient: Well-organized, using resources carefully.
inspiration: The reason you do something creative.
intern: An entry-level position for young people to gain experience.

CHAPTER ONE

Childhood Fascination

Jack Dorsey is more than just a successful ***entrepreneur***; he is an innovator. Innovative people find ways to make something new and useful using tools that already exist. As a master programmer and ***dispatch enthusiast***, Jack combined his two interests to invent something new: a way to communicate online using short strings of text. Twitter posts only allow users to write up to 140 characters, or letters, per post.

Later on, Jack thought about other ways to make the world a better place. While people had been using credit cards online and in large retail stores for years, there was no way for small merchants to charge customers on the go. Jack came up with the idea that led to Square, an ***application*** for smartphones that allows merchants to swipe credit cards using a piece

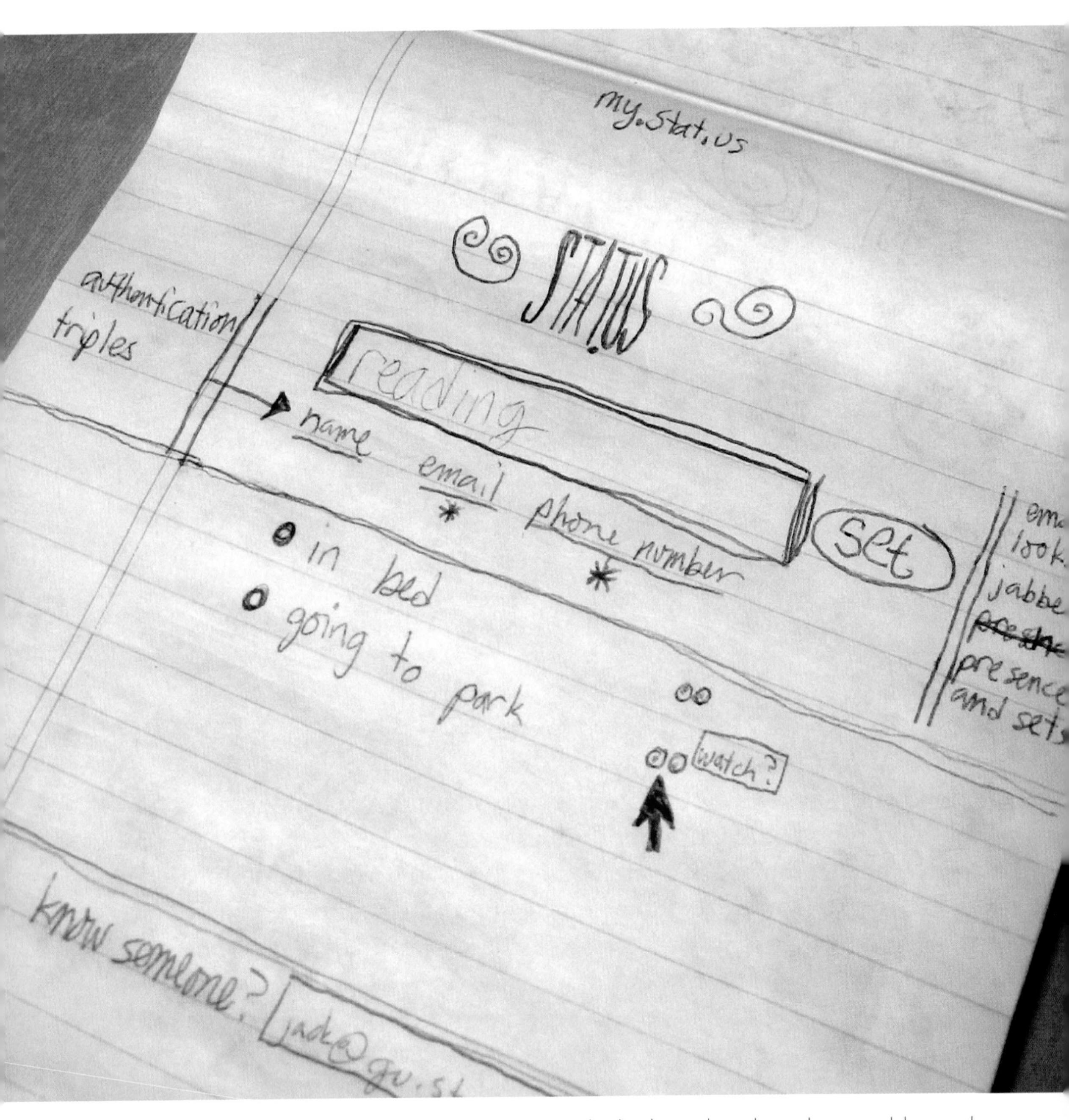

These are Jack Dorsey's notes as he began to think about the ideas that would one day become Twitter.

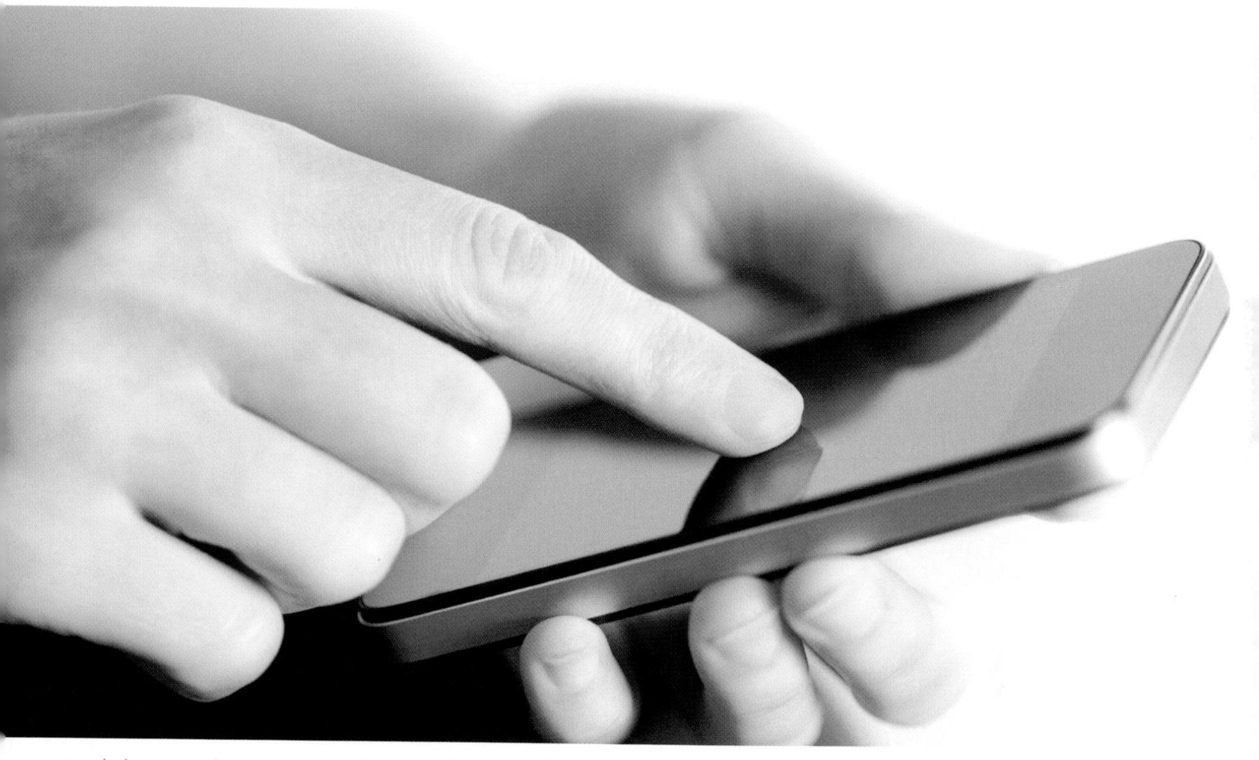

Jack knows that the popularity of smartphones is creating new opportunities for businesses like Twitter and his new company, Square Inc.

of hardware attached to the phone. Customers can then sign with their finger on the phone's screen and be on their way.

More recently, Jack took his ideas with digital purchasing a step further when he invented Square Wallet. Like the original Square, Square Wallet is a tool people can use to purchase items in a simpler way. It links users' credit card information to their smartphones so they can purchase items without ever needing to take out their credit card. Like Square, this invention makes processing a purchase take less time than ever before.

For all of his contributions to technological advancement, Jack was given

10 TWITTER

It may seem strange, but the man who helped create the world's latest method of communication had a lot of trouble expressing himself and communicating with others as a young man.

Make Connections: Origin of Twitter

Although the word Twitter is now most well known as a social media website, it is also a word that means "a short burst of inconsequential information," and "chirps from birds." This explains why the logo for Twitter is a songbird, and the name of a Twitter update is a "tweet."

the Innovator of the Year Award in 2012. In an article released by *Forbes* that same year, he was compared to another great entrepreneur: Steve Jobs, the founder of Apple. According to the article, Jack "is nerdier than Steve Jobs," even if his "ego seems in check."

When Jack found out about this comparison, he was insulted. "I think the reference was because I am a programmer, so if that is the nerdy way, then guilty: I am a nerd," he explained. Programmers write pieces of code that tell a computer how to behave. Because Jack did all of the programming himself, Twitter expanded rapidly.

The man who created the ***revolutionary*** tools known as Twitter and Square did not have a typical childhood. He overcame many trials to become the successful entrepreneur he is today. Jack was not the best communicator in his youth, so communicating via text rather than with his voice came naturally to him. As an adult, he used his childhood challenges to help him find ways to help people around the world interact with each other in simpler, clearer ways than ever before.

EARLY YEARS

Jack Dorsey was born on November 19, 1976, in St. Louis, Missouri. As a young boy, he found it very hard to communicate with his family and fellow students due to a speech ***impediment***. "I could pronounce [words]

Jack Dorsey was born in St. Louis, Missouri, and most of his growing-up years were spent in the St. Louis region.

in my head, but they just would not come out," he explained. Jack naturally shied away from making friends and spent most of his time at home. Fortunately, he had two younger brothers to keep him company.

As Jack grew older, it became apparent that he needed help. His parents brought him to a speech therapist to help him learn how to speak properly. Jack seized the opportunity to improve. He combated his shyness by entering contests that required him to give speeches to an audience. Some speeches could be prepared while others needed to be ***impromptu***.

Even with all of the help Jack was getting, he spent a lot of time at home because he did not feel entirely comfortable speaking with others. "That has always held me back a little, in terms of speaking up immediately," he has said. "I want to make sure that every word is perfectly said." Jack's experiences as a child greatly influenced who he became as he grew older. Even as an adult, he admits, "I can be silent at some times, which unsettles people a bit because they don't know what I'm thinking."

UNDERSTANDING HIS SURROUNDINGS

Jack and his family moved around a lot while he was growing up. Jack's father, who was an engineer specializing in medical devices, changed jobs frequently, which meant his family often moved their home. Mostly, they lived around St. Louis, but there was a time when they lived as far west as Denver, Colorado.

Every time his family moved to a new neighborhood, Jack pushed himself to go outside and explore his new surroundings. Knowing how to fend for himself was important to Jack, especially considering the difficulty he had speaking and leaving he house as a child. According to his mother, "Maybe it was a self-defense thing. He was trying to find his way around and feel comfortable in different areas."

The way Jack traveled varied greatly. Sometimes he would take public transportation and at other times he would walk around for hours at a time. He was particularly fascinated with vehicles and the way they moved from

When Jack was young, he loved to keep track of trains and their networks of tracks.

one place to another. It was not uncommon for Jack to bring his younger brothers down to the local train yard just to take pictures of the trains that were parked there. During a trip to Europe, he took hundreds of pictures of trains and payphones.

COMPUTERS AND COMMUNICATION

When Jack wasn't exploring the city, he focused on the technology lying around the house. His father's job as an engineer gave Jack access to computers before most of the other kids his age. He first began playing with computers at the age of eight, but merely using computers was not enough for him; he wanted to understand how computers worked!

Jack taught himself how to build computer programs at a time when his fellow students didn't even know how to use a computer. All this took place before he was even a teenager. Jack's fascination with trains went hand-in-hand with his interest in technology. He decorated his room with posters of maps and trains, all the while thinking about how the city was connected in one large grid.

Jack has said that if he hadn't become so interested in computers, he might have become an urban planner instead. He began tracking the movement of police cars and other emergency vehicles using public information from the Internet and a special computer program he wrote himself. "Suddenly, I had this very rich picture of what the city was doing," he explained in an interview. "I just wanted screens and screens of these things all around my room."

Monitoring what was happening around town on computer screens was fun, but Jack wanted to get to the heart of how vehicles moved and communicated. He used a police scanner to pick up radio signals transmitted from emergency vehicles moving through his area of town. The way the people in the vehicles communicated with one another fascinated Jack. "They're always talking about where they're going, what they're doing, and where they currently are," he said.

Computers made dispatchers' jobs much easier. These dispatchers use short phrases to communicate vital information to people in emergency situations. Their way of communicating would eventually help Jack come up with the ideas behind Twitter.

The people Jack listened to on the police scanner did not speak in full sentences. Instead, they used short codes to communicate what was happening. Jack thought this was very ***efficient***, and began thinking of ways these short bursts of communication could be used in other areas of life. The signals Jack listened to through his police scanner became his very first ***inspiration*** for the future creation of Twitter.

FIRST JOB

Jack was far ahead of the curve when it came to working. He started his first job as a programmer at Mira Digital Publishing just after entering high school, when he was fifteen years old.

When Jack joined Mira Digital Publishing, he was eager to introduce himself to the owner of the company, Jim McKelvey, on his first day. Jack tapped Jim on the shoulder to say hello, and Jim responded by saying he would get back to Jack in a moment. Then, Jim turned around and became so involved in his work that he forgot Jack was standing there. It was a full forty-five minutes before Jim turned around to find Jack standing there, waiting patiently for Jim to give him a moment of his time. Later, Jim always remembered that moment—but at the time, it was Jack's programming skills that truly impressed him.

Jack developed a reputation for getting all his work done quickly, and making his programs perform exactly as Jim requested. His attention to detail eventually led him to manage people twice his age even when he was just an ***intern***. Jim McKelvey was so humbled by Jack's work that he once referred to himself as the "assistant to the summer intern," implying that he was the assistant to Jack, a fifteen-year-old!

COLLEGE AND BEYOND

Jack greatly valued education and learning, so he never had any doubt that he would attend college. He graduated from a Catholic high school in St. Louis and then moved on to a university in Rolla, Missouri. The

Text-Dependent Questions

1. Which award did Jack Dorsey earn in 2012?
2. What difficulties did Jack face as a child, and what were some of the ways he both overcame and used these difficulties as he grew older?
3. According to Jack's mother, why did he spend so much time exploring the neighborhood as a child?
4. When did Jack first start learning how to create computer programs, and what kinds of programs did he create?
5. What are some of the ways Jack impressed Jim McKelvey at the age of fifteen?
6. How was Jack able to obtain the contact information of the dispatch company in New York?

Missouri University of Science and Technology became his new home, but he did not stay there long.

Thinking ahead is one of Jack's strengths. Even when he was still in college, he was already looking at future job prospects. He found the website of a dispatch company in New York City and thought about applying. Unfortunately, there was just one problem: the public website did not include a way to contact the company!

Many people would just give up and try to find another company to work for, but not Jack! He used his skills to get the contact information he couldn't find on the public webpage. "I found a way into the website. I found a security hole," he explained. Using the flaw he found in the website's programming, he was able to enter the full website through a backdoor and retrieve the information he needed. Technically, this is known as

Research Project

Jack Dorsey has said his inspiration for Twitter came from the strings of voice communication he heard over the police scanner as a child. Research the difference between dispatch language and Twitter posts and explain how they are both similar and different. Is it possible that dispatchers may use Twitter-like computer programs in the future?

hacking, but Jack did not do it to cause any harm. He just wanted to find a way to contact the company.

After Jack retrieved some e-mail addresses from the website, he decided to do the right thing and notify the company of the weakness he found. He sent an e-mail to the company saying, "You have a security hole. Here's how to fix it. Also, I write dispatch software." The company was so impressed with Jack's actions that they hired him a week later.

According to Jack, landing a job at a dispatch company in New York was a "dream come true." He packed up his bags and moved halfway across the country, where he continued pursuing his college degree at New York University. He was only nineteen years old at the time, but he was already thinking big.

Words to Understand

resources: A supply of money, staff, and other things a company can use to get things done.

technology: Something that humans invent to make something easier or do something new.

functionality: The range of different things a computer program can do.

investment: Money that you put into a company, hoping that the company will profit so you can make money from it.

acquired: Added to another company.

asset: Something useful.

market research: Research done to see what things people want to use or buy.

spam: Junk mail or online messages that are annoying.

self-promotion: Advertising yourself to try to get more customers.

CHAPTER TWO

Introducing Twitter

The dispatch company Jack worked for, which was founded by Greg Kidd, began expanding while Jack pursued his degree at New York University. Jack continued to write dispatch software for Dispatch Management Services Corp. for several years during this time. In 2000, Greg decided to branch out to other areas of the United States. He started a web-based dispatch company known as dNet.com and asked for Jack's help with the website.

Not long after, Jack started his own company and moved to California. He followed in the footsteps of many young entrepreneurs before him and dropped out of college before graduating. There was no reason for him to stay in school, he thought, if he already knew everything he needed to know to start his own company and move forward in his life. Finally, he had the ***resources*** and time to work on projects of his own.

Jack made the right decision when he chose to move to California. Greg's new website failed, so it was a good thing that James had started

Eventually, Twitter became so popular and successful that even the President of the United States is a Twitter user. Here President Barack Obama uses Twitter to hold a live question-and-answer session in the Roosevelt Room of the White House in December 2012.

his own company. His company dispatched couriers, taxis, and emergency services using the Internet. But it wasn't making Jack much money, so he tried out several different jobs over the next few years. He even spent some time studying massage therapy! None of the jobs he had felt like the right fit, though.

TWITTER

Jack began to think about how ***technology*** could be used to improve the world. He reflected on the dispatch conversations he listened to as a child and thought of ways to apply that thinking to the Internet, which was now expanding rapidly. When he began working for a podcasting company in 2005, his dreams began to take shape.

Jack saw a clear connection between the Internet and the increasing use of cell phones. "Now, we all have these cell phones. We had text messaging. Suddenly we could update where I was, what I'm doing, where I'm going, how I feel. And then it would go out to the entire world," he said in an interview. At the time, smartphones were uncommon and just starting to come out. If Jack wanted to connect everyday people to the Internet through cell phones, he would need to do it through text messages.

Jack wasted no time pitching his new idea to his new employer, Odeo. One former executive recounted the experience: "He came to us with this idea: 'What if you could share your status with all your friends really easily, so they know what you're doing'?" Odeo, the company that hired Jack, was interested in his idea for Twitter, which he referred to as "twttr" when the project first began.

The short name, which is credited to Noah Glass, came from the current trend at the time to keep abbreviations short. When users received a text from Twitter, it would be distributed from the abbreviation twttr, and the SMS code 40404. Developers of the website hoped the code would be easy for users to memorize and recognize.

Jack received help for his new project from Biz Stone, Odeo's creative director, and another contractor named Florian Weber. All three were very talented programmers, and they were able to build the first version of Twitter within two weeks. On March 21, 2006, Jack sent out his first Twitter update, known as a tweet. It said, "just setting up my twttr." Only Odeo employees used the first version of Twitter, as it was not ready to be shared with the world.

Jack Dorsey (right) with Twitter's cofounder Evan Williams (left).

Make Connections: Short Messages

Twitter has restricted users to 140 character messages since it first began. Jack always envisioned that Twitter should be restricted to short messages, but the real reason he limited Twitter posts to exactly 140 characters is so that they could be sent and delivered using just one text message. At the time, text messages were limited to anywhere between 140 and 160 characters each. Even though SMS messaging has changed since Twitter first began, Twitter's restriction has not. All tweets are still only allowed to be 140 characters or less in length.

The developers of Twitter spent a lot of money testing the ***functionality*** of the website. Having an unlimited text message plan was almost unheard of at the time, so they were forced to pay for each individual text message that was sent or received during testing. They racked up thousands of dollars in SMS charges to their phones during this time. Fortunately, this ***investment*** would eventually prove that it was all worth it.

Everything began to change starting in July 2006 when Twitter was released publicly. It took off very slowly at first, but it showed a lot of promise. Jack Dorsey, Biz Stone, and Evan Williams created a new company, which they named Obvious Corporation. They also ***acquired*** Odeo and every ***asset*** Odeo owned. One year later, Twitter branched off as its own company.

GAINING USERS

Jack and his team were finding it hard to get people to use Twitter, and the reasons were obvious. Evan Williams, one of Jack's partners, explained why in a 2013 interview: "With Twitter, it wasn't clear what

Twitter's third cofounder, Biz Stone.

Make Connections: Rapid Growth

At the start of 2007, there were 400,000 tweets posted per quarter of the year. By 2008, one hundred million tweets were posted per quarter. By 2011, 140 million tweets were posted daily, and the website has continued to grow ever since.

it was," he began. "They called it a social network, they called it microblogging, but it was hard to define, because it didn't replace anything. There was this path of discovery with something like that, where over time you figure out what it is."

Evan Williams was correct; Jack and his team needed to figure out exactly how users would see Twitter before they began advertising it. That moment came in 2007, at the South by Southwest Interactive Conference. This large conference features emerging technology that has not yet gained popularity in the world. It is known to foster great ideas for the future. Many innovators like Jack Dorsey go to this conference each year.

Twitter was right at home at the South by Southwest Interactive Conference. Jack and his team set up computer monitors where attendees could monitor the tweets of other users. The service was mentioned by panelists and speakers, which greatly increased the amount of people who used Twitter during the conference. Tweets tripled from 20,000 per day to 60,000 per day while the conference took place. At the end of the conference, Twitter received the Web Award.

Many of Twitter's first users were everyday people talking about their lives, but the service caught on quickly. It didn't take more than a year before celebrities and other famous people began using the service for their own needs. Both 2008 presidential candidates, Barack Obama and John

McCain, used Twitter to keep in touch with their supporters while campaigning. And later, they used another invention of Jack Dorsey: Square.

THE MANY USES OF TWITTER

In 2009, a ***market research*** company did a study to figure out exactly how people were using Twitter. The research found that 40 percent of tweets were about "pointless babble." Another 38 percent were conversational tweets between users. Only 4 percent of posts were about news, with another 4 percent being taken up by ***spam*** posts. Six percent of posts involved ***self-promotion***, while nine percent of tweets were retweeted to pass along information.

Expanding websites are prone to outages, or periods of time where the website is simply overloaded with users and cannot function properly, causing the website to crash. Twitter's rapid growth from 2007 to 2008 led to many of these outages, and the service has experienced periodic outages ever since. Fortunately, these outages only occur a few times a year, and they are usually due to an unusual spike in activity. Regular maintenance is performed to expand Twitter's servers as the website continues to grow.

One of the ways people use Twitter is to discuss current events. This is a great way to pass on information long before others can catch it on the news or any other social media website. The servers that host Twitter undergo more strain during a very popular event, such as a large sports game or media award show. These events can temporarily shut the servers down for minutes or even hours.

As Twitter grew on an international level, people were using the service to share their experiences with users from across the world. In 2009, many Iranian people were using Twitter to communicate with each other about ongoing protests in the country. Twitter had planned to have a scheduled maintenance during this time, but a United States State Department spokesperson asked Twitter to delay the maintenance so that people in Iran could communicate—and Twitter agreed!

Make Connections: Retweeting

One of the ways users can pass along information is by retweeting someone else's tweet. At first, there was no official way to differentiate a unique tweet from a retweet, so users would prefix a repost with the short code: rt. Twitter eventually added in the functionality to differentiate between unique and reposted tweets so that users did not have to mark retweets themselves.

Thanks to Twitter, the whole world is now linked together in one large network. All users have to do is type a short 140 character tweet! "Now I can see the entire world, and how they're thinking, and how they're feeling, and what they're doing, and what they care about, and where they're going," Jack Dorsey said in an interview. Twitter became exactly what he hoped it would be.

Although Twitter has many possible uses, most users use it as a microblogging service. In other words, they post small snippets about their day on Twitter for their followers to see. They might talk about how they are feeling about an upcoming test, what they are eating at the moment, or what movie they plan to see later on tonight. This is exactly how Jack envisioned the average person would use Twitter when he created Twitter in the first place.

Jack was once asked about his proudest moment regarding the invention of Twitter. He said, "I am most proud of how quickly people came to it and used it in a million different ways." People are finding different ways to use Twitter each day.

USERS SHAPE THE FUTURE

Twitter users have greatly defined how Twitter is used, but they have also inspired new functionality within the website. For example, users began

Research Project

Twitter has changed a lot over the years, but its basic idea has mostly stayed the same. Using the Internet, research how Twitter has changed since it was first released to the public in 2007. List three ways the website has improved and explain where you think Twitter should focus its efforts in the future.

using hashtags long before they were officially supported by Twitter. Hashtags were invented as a way to communicate ideas within text. They are created by typing a pound symbol followed by any combination of words. One example of a hashtag would be #hashtag.

These hashtags were used to explain what a post was about in as little characters as possible. After all, users only had 140 characters to work with! A user posting about food might put #food at the end of a post. At first, these hashtags were only text markings and could not be interacted with in any other way. This all changed in July of 2009 when hashtags were officially adopted by Twitter.

From that point forward, any hashtag became a link that users could click to view any other posts that contained the same hashtag. It was an easy way to search for people who were talking about the same thing, and it made the Twitter community feel more connected than ever before. In 2012, Twitter introduced the cashtag, which is a dollar sign followed by a combination of words, to allow users to track companies and their stocks. One example of a cashtag is $twitter.

Twitter is not a typical social media website. Users do not add each other as friends. Instead, they follow each other's Twitter accounts. Long before users could physically link to other users using a similar functionality to hashtags, they came up with a way of their own to communicate

Text-Dependent Questions

1. Why did Jack Dorsey decide to drop out of college and move to California?
2. When Jack first approached Odeo about Twitter, how did he pitch his idea?
3. Why was Twitter only available to Odeo employees at first? When was the site finally introduced to the public?
4. How did the South by Southwest Interactive Conference cause Twitter to grow at a much faster rate?
5. According to the study done in 2009, what are the top three uses for Twitter?
6. What are hashtags used for?

with each other. All usernames were prefixed with the @ symbol to show that they were trying to communicate with a specific user. Twitter eventually added functionality for this, with the @username now linking to the user account it mentioned.

Some other websites have adopted the use of hashtags and linking usernames, also using # and @. One popular website that followed Twitter's lead is Facebook. With 900 million unique monthly visitors, Facebook is the only social media website to be more popular than Twitter. Jack Dorsey's creation boasts 310 million unique monthly visitors. LinkedIn is not far behind with 250 million unique monthly visitors.

Jack had come up with an amazing idea—but he had more ideas up his sleeve!

Words to Understand

chief executive officer: The highest-ranking person in charge of running a company.

inception: The moment when you have an idea for something.

CHAPTER THREE

Inventing Square

By 2008, Twitter was really taking off. According to Jack, "We'd raised $20 million, and the servers were crashing every day." The website was growing faster than anyone could have imagined, but that was a good thing! "It wasn't so much that the ship was sinking," Jack commented, "but more 'Great job, Jack—we've got to up our level of experience and lay some foundation for a much bigger organization."

Unfortunately, Jack never got the chance to improve the company in the ways he envisioned. His job as ***chief executive officer*** (CEO) was taken away in October 2008 when Twitter co-founder Evan Williams asked Jack to step down from his CEO position. After Jack agreed, Evan

Jack's next idea was Square, an actual little square that could plug into smartphones.

took over the position for himself. This experience absolutely crushed Jack. "It was like being punched in the stomach," he explained.

Despite the pain he felt, Jack ultimately understood why he was removed from his management position. He explained by saying, "I left myself be in a weird position because it always felt like Ev's company. He funded it. He was the chairman. And I was this new guy who was a programmer, who had an idea. I would not be strong in my convictions, basically, because he was the older, wiser one."

Both men had their strengths and weaknesses. Jack was better at coming up with ideas and creating new products, while Evan was better at managing people and directing a large, growing company. Jack understood his weaknesses, but he believed the whole situation could have been avoided if Jack and Evan had been more direct with one another while they worked together. "Communication was number one, internally and externally. We could have done a much better job, and me personally," he said.

Jack did not completely cut ties with Twitter once he was replaced. He was still a board member, but he was no longer working for the company as an employee. It may have been hard to see at the time, but being removed from his management role at Twitter did have its advantages. Jack was now free to work on other ideas and new projects. He didn't let the experience get him down. It only took one year for him to become invested in a new idea that became immensely successful: Square!

INSPIRATION FOR SQUARE

Despite all of his success with Twitter, Jack had kept in touch with his first boss from St. Louis over the years. Jim McKelvey was now working as a glass artisan. He sold his pieces individually at fairs and other events. One day, he called Jack to complain about a lost sale that could have been prevented if a program like Square existed at the time.

In an interview, Jack explained how Square got started: "[Jim] was

Square allows users to turn their iPhones into cash registers.

Jack's idea for Square would help artists take credit cards when selling their art at art festivals and craft fairs, but many other small business people would be able to benefit from Jack's next big idea as well.

at an art fair, and he couldn't sell a piece of glass because he couldn't accept a credit card. So, that was $2,000 lost, and he just got fed up with that. He came out to San Francisco that next week and we spent the week trying to figure out why no one has done this before."

Progress on Square started out slow. Jack and Jim had a simple idea of what it would be, and it was all based on Jim's experience as a small merchant. If Jim were able to accept credit card information while working at the art fair, he wouldn't have lost the $2,000 sale. That was the problem the two men worked to solve. "It was a way to accept credit cards on your phone. That's all we knew," Jack said.

Square has had great success as smartphones and tablet computers become even more popular.

Make Connections: Name

Jack and Jim had a little bit of trouble coming up with a name for what would eventually be known as Square. At first, Jack wanted to give the application a name having to do with squirrels due to the way squirrels gather nuts and bring them back home, similar to how merchants would gather payments all in one place. When he realized there was already a company with the name Squirrel Systems, he knew he couldn't use the squirrel idea anymore. He opened a dictionary and looked for names similar to squirrel, and found square. He liked the word square because it could be used as a term to say, "We're even," or, "We're squared away," when people were talking about money. The card reader used to take payments is also shaped like a square.

At the time of Square's ***inception***, smartphones were just starting to become popular. Surfing on the Internet with these new phones was easy. New applications—or apps—were constantly being released to make everyday life simpler. Both Jack and Jim had iPhones, and they decided smartphones would be the key to their new invention. An application for the smartphone would make it possible to pay for goods or services in all sorts of situations, whether it be for merchants at an art fair or everyday people selling items at a garage sale.

CREATING THE APPLICATION

The first version of Square was being developed for Apple products. Apple had to approve all the applications included on the iPhone first, so Jack and Jim sought out an interview with an executive at Apple. They managed to meet with Scott Forstall, the senior vice president of development, as well as a few other members of his team.

With big businesses like Starbucks using Square, Jack's new company was on its way to amazing success.

Make Connections: Square Register

The advantages of using Square do not stop at the location it is used. Even some retail stores have begun using the Square Register application, which essentially turns an iPad into an improved cash register. The difference between a Square Register and a cash register is what information the two registers keep track of. While all cash registers keep track of total sales made, Square Registers analyze data and can keep track of what items were sold and how many of each item were sold. The information gathered through Square Register can be used to help merchants better understand what items are in demand and when.

The company Square, Inc., was founded in 2009, but it wasn't until 2010 that the first application was officially released because development took a long time. A small card reader was needed to use the program, and it would be plugged in via the smartphone's audio jack. Jack took care of the programming of the server that would take the payment information, while Jim worked on the hardware that would be used to read the credit cards. They teamed up with Tristan O'Tierney, who worked on programming the iPhone app itself.

Using the application is very simple. All the merchant has to do is input the price on the screen and have customers swipe their card. Signing a receipt is equally easy; all users have to do is sign their name onscreen. The process takes less than a few seconds, and is as easy to use as any other retail card reader.

Square filled the gap that Jack and Jim felt was missing from the modern technological world. Although the app was designed with small merchants in mind, it has been picked up by larger companies as well.

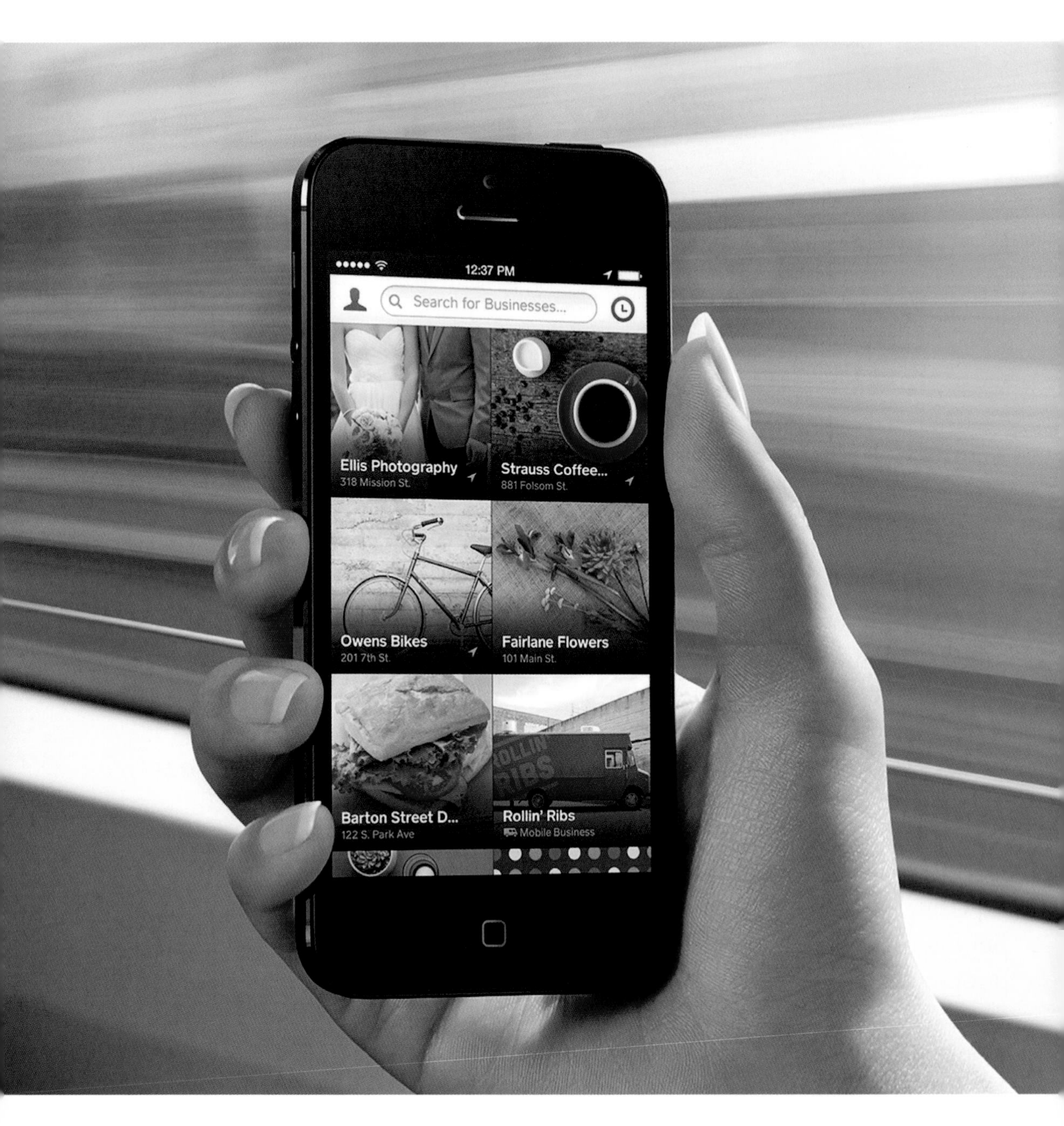

Using the Square Wallet means you don't have to use an actual credit card to make purchases on your account.

Text-Dependent Questions

1. Why was Jack forced out of his CEO position at Twitter in 2008?
2. What caused Jack Dorsey and Jim McKelvey to come up with the idea that would eventually become Square?
3. What process did Jack go through when picking a name for Square and why did he settle on the name he did?
4. Who were the three men who worked on the functionality of Square and what were their three separate roles?
5. What are some of the advantages of using a Square Register instead of any other cash register?
6. How does Square Wallet help both customers and merchants make faster transactions than ever before?

In 2012, Starbucks announced it would be using Square for all its credit or debit transactions. Companies like Apple have been using Square for a long time already.

OTHER VERSIONS

Square, Inc. has branched off in many different directions over the years. Square Wallet puts even more emphasis on smartphones than even Square did. It cuts out the need for a credit card altogether, because people who use Square Wallet can store their payment information on their smartphone and share it with the merchant automatically. Square Wallet is currently used on Android and Apple phones.

According to Jack, "Money touches every single person on the planet," so Square is useful for everyone who would like their money transactions to go just a little bit smoother. Square released a few new, innovative

The Square Stand added yet another convenient feature to Square.

Research Project

Square, Inc., has released a lot of different services since it was first founded in 2009. Using the Internet, research Jack Dorsey's latest inventions. Do they have anything to do with Square or has he branched off into another direction? Explain how you believe his newest inventions will help the world become more connected.

services in 2013. Square Cash uses e-mail to exchange money from one person to another, while Square Market allows sellers to set up a digital storefront to sell their merchandise.

The hardware used to support Square is constantly being improved. The Square Stand, also released in 2013, makes it easier for the Apple iPad to accept transactions. The service has been expanded to include other countries. Square was first made available in Canada in 2012 and Japan in 2013. Square will likely be made available in many more countries in the years to come.

Words to Understand

serendipity: Luck or chance.

stocks: Shares of a company, which people can buy and sell.

implementing: Putting into practice.

velocity: Speed.

CHAPTER FOUR

Climbing Higher

Jack began his climb to success by picking up his life and moving to New York City before he was even twenty years old. He made a bold move when he warned a dispatch company of a security hole in their website, which could have gotten him into a lot of trouble. Bold moves are Jack's trademark; they're what set Jack apart from other inventors. He is willing to take risks that might lead to success or failure. Fortunately for him, almost all his big moves have led to success.

UNCONVENTIONAL BOSS

Jack has never been a typical boss. He doesn't work at a desk and instead uses an iPad to get his work done. In an attempt to learn from the

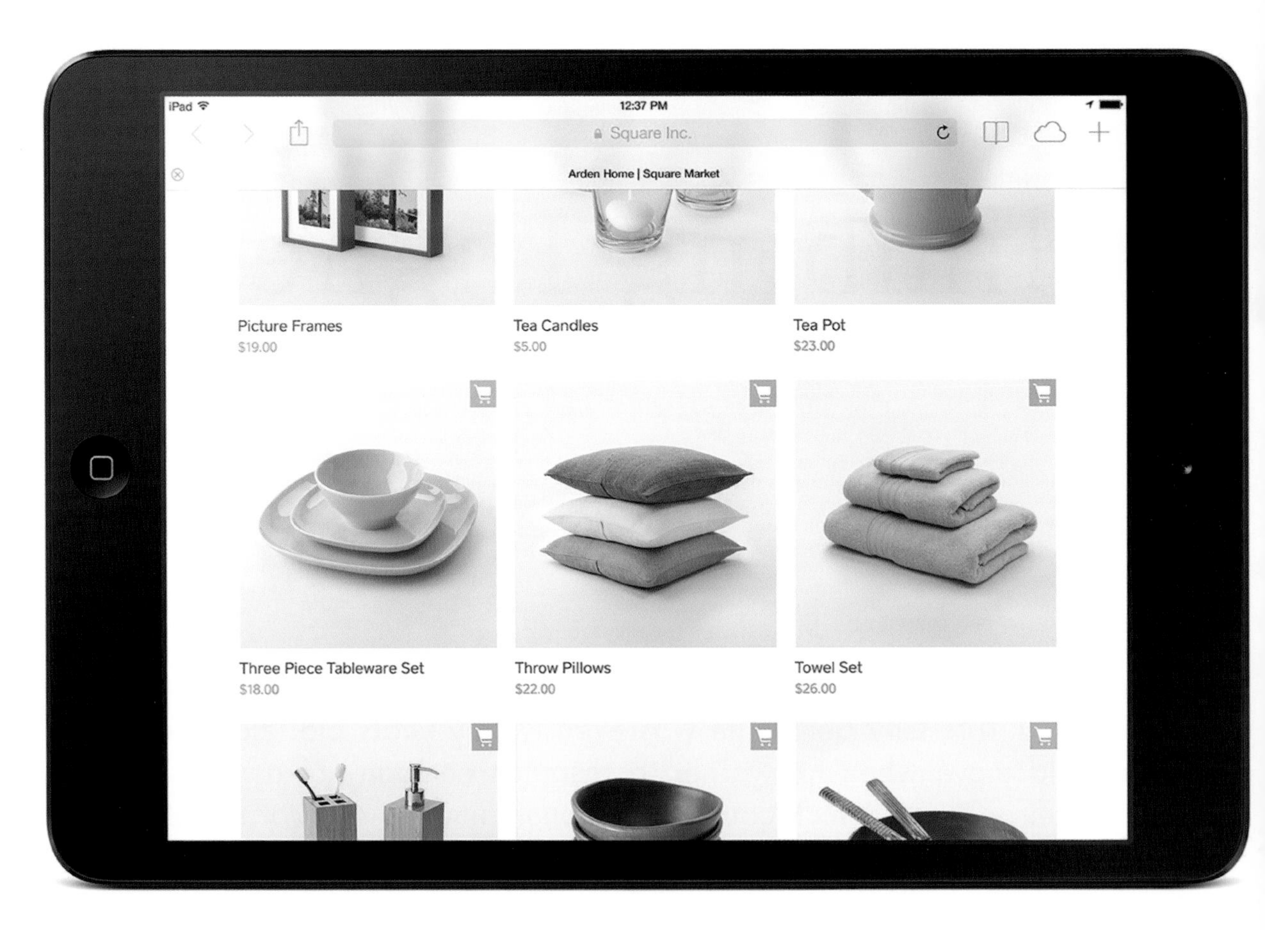

Square is continuing to add new features, such as Square Market, which allows users to set up a digital store to sell their products.

Make Connections: Continued Growth

Although well established, Twitter and Square are far from finished. Twitter now boasts over 170 million registered users, some of which are very influential people such as celebrities and politicians. Its ease of use and accessibility make it the perfect tool for anyone in the world. Both Twitter and Square are available to anyone who has a smartphone or a computer, which is becoming more common with each passing year. In 2010, the first tweet was sent from the International Space Station, in space. Since then, at least a dozen tweets are sent to the Earth from space each day.

mistakes he made as Twitter's CEO, he does his best to communicate directly with his employees at Square. Jack explained in an interview that one of his greatest challenges was learning how to come out of his shell socially. "The biggest thing I've learned is that I need to communicate more; I need to be more vocal," he explained, and he is doing everything in his power to improve.

Jack is known to roam around the office to talk to people. He is very transparent with his employees, which means he tells them his goals for the company's future upfront. There are very little secrets within Square, Inc. E-mails are sent out to the entire team of hundreds of employees on a regular basis.

Jack's need for an open work environment goes both ways. "We encourage people to stay out in the open because we believe in ***serendipity***—and people walking by each other teaching new things," he explained. He hopes to train all his employees to embrace the open, connected atmosphere that Square has become.

The Twitter logo hangs on the front of the New York Stock Exchange on the day of Twitter's Initial Public Offering (IPO).

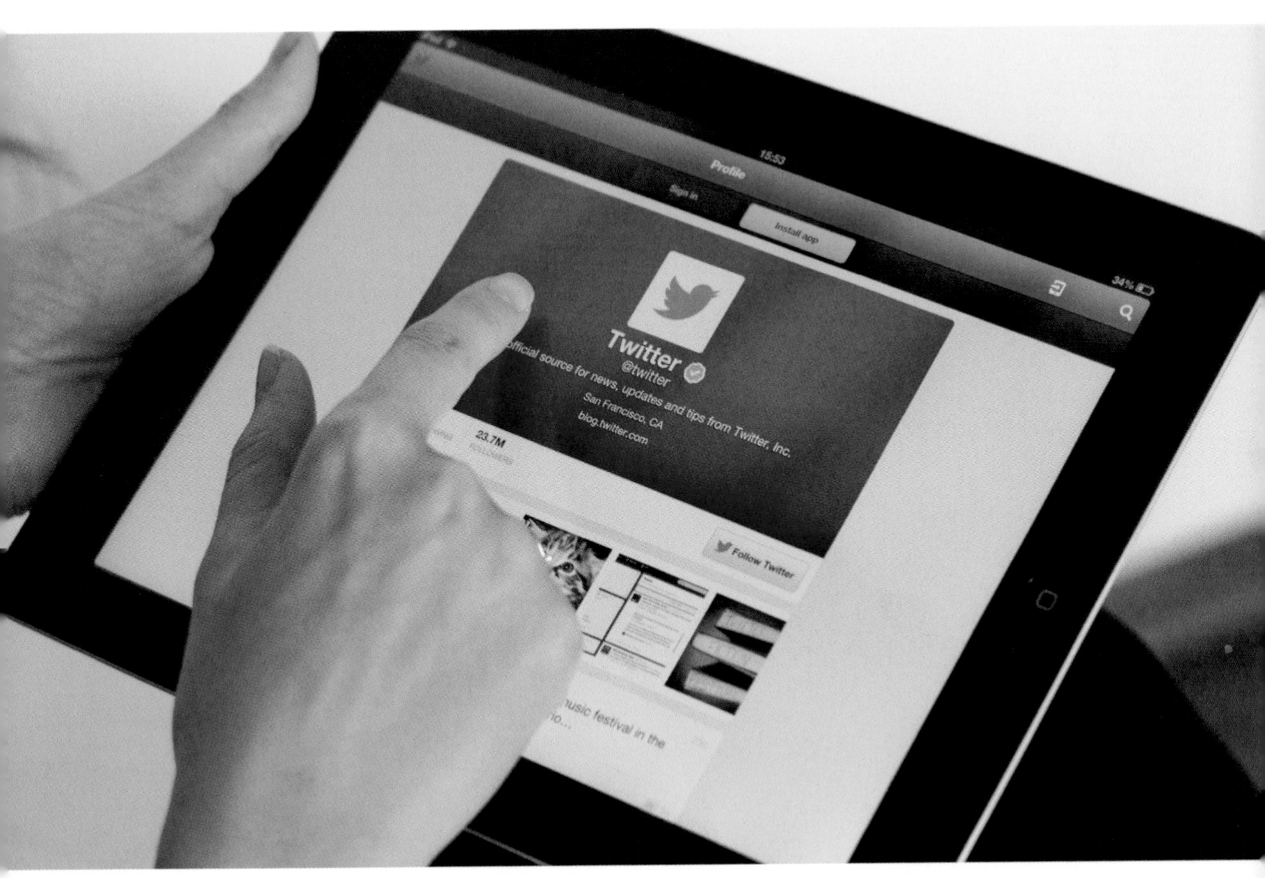

Twitter has only become more popular since Jack left the company, with new users creating accounts everyday and millions of users tweeting all the time, including on new mobile platforms like the iPad.

Jack became a billionaire in 2013 when Square was valued at more than $3 billion. In 2014, Jack was estimated as being worth more than $2 billion on his own. Part of the reason his worth jumped so quickly is due to Twitter's decision to be traded publicly. Although Jack did not work directly for the company at the time, he still owned part of it. The first ***stocks*** were expected to trade at $26 each during Twitter's Initial

For Jack, the Golden Gate Bridge is a symbol of how something that is truly beautiful can also be an efficient and practical tool to make humans' lives easier.

Public Offering (IPO), but quickly jumped in price to $45 because of Twitter's popularity. Lots of people were buying shares! Jack owns more than 23 million shares on his own, which gives him over one billion dollars just from Twitter!

Despite Jack's immense success, he doesn't let his money get to his head. One of his biggest pieces of advice to young entrepreneurs is this: "The strongest thing you can cultivate as an entrepreneur is to not rely on luck but cultivating an ability to recognize fortunate situations when they are occurring."

By paying attention to his surroundings, Jack was able to come up with ideas that would be very useful in the world but were not yet available. Making these ideas available before anyone else beat him to the punch is what brought him so much success. Getting there, however, was not always easy. In 2012, he released a list of rules for success. They are:

- Don't be a jerk.
- Don't take anyone for granted.
- Enjoy the moment.
- Be honest, always.
- Be humble.
- Be kind.
- Respect people's wishes.
- Allow endings.
- Fail openly.
- Have an amazing haircut.

Jack teaches his employees to see the world through his eyes by bringing them out into the real world to look at the Golden Gate Bridge in San Francisco. He explained in an interview that people do not think of the bridge's function when they are using it. But, when they gaze at it from afar, they admire how beautiful it is and how easily it gets its job done.

Jack is inspired by New York City's Mayor Bloomberg. One of Jack's next goals is to become mayor of New York City. Given his past track record, he may just make it!

"We see the bridge as like the perfect intersection between art and engineering. It has pure utility, in that people commute on it every single day," he explains.

Jack's admiration for the Golden Gate Bridge is very similar to the way he looked at trains and other modes of transportation as a child. He has always aimed to make his products as simple as possible. "When people come to Twitter and they want to express something in the world, the technology fades away," he says. "It's them writing a simple message and them knowing that people are going to see it."

JACK DORSEY'S FUTURE

When Jack first moved to New York City to work for Dispatch Management Services, Corp., he fell in love with the city. It was much busier than St. Louis, and he enjoyed watching the hustle and bustle of people moving around and finding their way. The bus systems and subway systems fascinated him, and he really wanted to understand exactly how everything worked. According to Jack, New York City is "kinda like being in a car in the middle of a thunderstorm. Everything is raging around you, but you're safe inside that car. So New York feels very much to me like that."

That passion never truly left Jack, even after he moved to California. He one day aspires to become the mayor of New York City and plans to follow in the footsteps of Mayor Michael Bloomberg, whom Jack sees as very similar to himself. "He comes from a technology background, a company background, a startup background," Jack explains. If Mayor Bloomberg was able to become the mayor, then Jack believes he might be able to as well!

Mayor Bloomberg has also taken notice of Jack and has supported him by saying, "Few people have been as successful at innovating—and ***implementing***—as Jack Dorsey." Michael Bloomberg was first elected

Jack has learned a lot since the days when he hung out watching trains—but he has stayed true to who he is.

Research Project

Jack Dorsey is a very ambitious person. Since Twitter went public in 2007, he has played a role in two very large and successful companies. Using the Internet, research Jack Dorsey's recent accomplishments. Is he doing anything outside business? Has he taken any steps closer to become New York City's new mayor?

in 2001 after having founded his own company just like Jack. "Could a tech entrepreneur really be elected mayor? That question is so 2001," he said. If Michael was able to become mayor, so could Jack!

Jack believes that New York City "is more influential in many cases than Capitol Hill," referring to the larger United States government. "With technology, you can have immediate impact. There's a ***velocity*** to it," he said.

Mayors play an important role in the management of a city, including how its public transportation and communication systems are managed. For Jack, becoming mayor of a large city like New York would be a dream come true.

Becoming mayor is still a long way off, but Jack Dorsey has found other pursuits to keep him occupied. He joined the board of directors of the Walt Disney Company in 2013, which would give him a say in the company's operations. His knowledge and understanding of the world's future needs will greatly help Disney, which is always looking for ways to improve on a technological level.

Jack has grown a lot since he was a young kid wandering around in train yards in his neighborhood, but his need to roam has remained.

Text-Dependent Questions

1. What are some of the ways Jack has tried to improve his communication skills since stepping down as Twitter's CEO?
2. Explain how Twitter's Initial Public Offering (IPO) increased Jack's wealth significantly.
3. What does Jack mean when he says, "The strongest thing you can cultivate as an entrepreneur is to not rely on luck but cultivating an ability to recognize fortunate situations when they are occurring?"
4. Explain why Jack takes new employees to the Golden Gate Bridge in San Francisco. What is he trying to teach them?
5. Why does Jack have such an interest in becoming the mayor of New York City?

When working on a new project, Jack prefers to spend his time alone with his thoughts. "The best thinking time is just walking," he explained.

He proves that not every successful businessman needs to be loud and talkative! Sometimes, they can be quiet and thoughtful—and still make a strong impact on the world.

FIND OUT MORE

In Books

Bilton, Nick. *Hatching Twitter: A True Story of Money, Power, Friendship, and Betrayal.* New York: Portfolio, 2013.

Fitton, Laura, Michael E. Gruen, and Leslie Poston. *Twitter for Dummies.* Hoboken, N.J.: Wiley, 2010.

Rosenberg, Scott. *Say Everything: How Blogging Began, What It's Becoming, and Why It Matters.* New York: Three Rivers, 2009.

Smith, Chris, and Marci McGrath. *Twitter: Jack Dorsey, Biz Stone and Evan Williams.* Greensboro: Morgan Reynolds, 2012.

Topper, Hilary. *Everything You Ever Wanted to Know about Social Media, but Were Afraid to Ask.* Bloomington, Ind.: Iuniverse, 2009.

On the Internet

Jack Dorsey
www.biography.com/people/jack-dorsey-578280

Jack Dorsey on the History of Twitter and Square
tusb.stanford.edu/2011/05/jack-dorsey-on-the-history-of-twitter-and-square.html

Profile Twitter Founders: Jack Dorsey, Biz Stone and Evan Williams
www.telegraph.co.uk/technology/twitter/4388880/Profile-Twitter-founders-Jack-Dorsey-Biz-Stone-and-Evan-Williams.html

The Real History of Twitter, In Brief
twitter.about.com/od/Twitter-Basics/a/The-Real-History-Of-Twitter-In-Brief.htm

Twitter Creator's Quest: Bring Order to Chaos
www.sfgate.com/news/article/Twitter-creator-s-quest-Bring-order-to-the-chaos-3176981.php

SERIES GLOSSARY OF KEY TERMS

application: A program that runs on a computer or smartphone. People often call these "apps."

bug: A problem with how a program runs.

byte: A unit of information stored on a computer. One byte is equal to eight digits of binary code—that's eight 1s or 0s.

cloud: Data and apps that are stored on the Internet instead of on your own computer or smartphone are said to be "in the cloud."

data: Information stored on a computer.

debug: Find the problems with an app or program and fix them.

device: Your computer, smartphone, or other piece of technology. Devices can often access the Internet and run apps.

digital: Having to do with computers or stored on a computer.

hardware: The physical part of a computer. The hardware is made up of the parts you can see and touch.

memory: Somewhere that a computer stores information that it is using.

media: Short for multimedia, it's the entertainment or information that can be stored on a computer. Examples of media include music, videos, and e-books.

network: More than one computer or device connected together so information can be shared between them.

pixel: A dot of light or color on a digital display. A computer monitor or phone screen has lots of pixels that work together to create an image.

program: A collection of computer code that does a job.

software: Programs that run on a computer.

technology: Something that people invent to make a job easier or do something new.

INDEX

ABOUT THE AUTHOR

Celicia Scott lives in upstate New York. She worked in teaching before starting a second career as a writer.

PICTURE CREDITS

6: David Shankbone
8: Jack Dorsey
16: FEMA, Jason Pack
20: Jack Dorsey
22: White House
24: Evan Williams
26: Joi
32: Andrew Mager
34: Square, Inc.
36: Square, Inc.
42: Square, Inc.
44: Square, Inc.
46: Walt Disney
48: Square, Inc.
52: MasterLu - Fotolia.com
56: Joi

9: Pressureua
10: Lucian Milasan
12: Rudi1976
14: Steven Jones
37: Ekaterina Bykova
38: Syda Productions
40: Robwilson39
50: Cpenler
51: Viorel Dudau
54: Laurence Agron